ON

W9-APX-834

JBIOG
Malco
Cwiklik, Robert

Malcolm X and Black Pride

MALCOLM X

and Black Pride

by Robert Cwiklik

Gateway Civil Rights
The Millbrook Press
Brookfield, Connecticut

Interior Design: Tilman Reitzle

Photographs courtesy of: Harvey Eisner: cover; Schomburg
Center for Research in Black Culture: cover inset, 2-3, 7, 10, 12,
14, 21, 29; AP/Wide World Photos: 1, 17 (bottom), 22-23, 26;
Russell Shorto: 4, 27, 28, 30; Steele Collection: 9; New-York
Historical Society: 17 (top); The Bettmann Archive: 19;
Moorland-Spingarn Research Center, Howard University: 24.

Cataloging-in-Publication Data

Cwiklik, Robert
Malcolm X and black pride.

32 pp.; ill.: (Gateway Civil Rights)
Bibliography: p.
Includes index.

Summary: Malcolm X was a leader of the Nation of Islam, a
movement to unite black people throughout the world. He taught
blacks to take pride in their race and to respect and help
themselves.
1. Malcolm X. 1925-1965. 2. Afro-Americans – Biography.
3. United States – race relations. 4. Civil rights workers.
1991 B (92) Malcolm X
ISBN 1-56294-042-2

Harlem in the 1940s.

When Malcolm Little was only 4 years old, he woke one night to the sounds of gunshots and screaming voices. He sat up in bed and began coughing. His eyes stung from the thick smoke and roaring flames that filled the house. It was like waking inside a furnace.

Malcolm tripped over his sister and brother as they all dashed out to escape the blaze. Outside, he saw his father, the Reverend Earl Little, aiming a rifle at a pair of fleeing men. Malcolm's mother herded the groggy children into the yard. She had barely made it outside, clutching Malcolm's baby brother to her, when the house came crashing down in a shower of sparks. The family stood in terrified silence as flames swallowed their home.

Two white men had set the fire. They did it because Malcolm's family was black, and this was a white neighborhood. Besides that, Malcolm's father was a minister who taught his black parishioners to have pride in themselves. Some local whites were frightened by his talk about blacks being a "mighty race." That was "uppity nigger" talk. The angry whites had decided to teach the Reverend Little a lesson. His son, young Malcolm Little, would never forget the terrible sight of the burning house.

This mural of Malcolm X's life adorns the
Audubon Ballroom in Harlem, New York.

Hard Years

Malcolm Little was born on May 19, 1925, in Omaha, Nebraska. In the decades following the Civil War, many blacks in America had moved to the Midwest and the North to get away from persecution in the South. The Civil War had ended slavery in the South, but blacks there were still treated very badly. They weren't allowed to vote, or to eat at the same lunch counter as white people, or to sit near them on the bus, or even to drink from the same water fountain. And they certainly couldn't live in the same nice neighborhoods and get the same good jobs as whites.

Many southern blacks were brutally beaten, or even murdered, if they didn't "remember their place." But those who moved to other parts of the country usually found that things weren't much better. White people forced them to live in the poorest neighborhoods and only allowed them to have the lowest kinds of jobs, such as shining shoes or washing dishes.

The Reverend Earl Little was a big, solid, dark-skinned man. Wherever he went, whites accused him of "spreading trouble" among the "good" blacks. Reverend Little taught that white people would never accept blacks as equals in America. He said that blacks would never be free until they moved back to the land of their origin—to Africa—where they could build their own great nation.

Earl Little had gotten these ideas from the writings of Marcus Garvey, the black man who founded the Back to Africa movement. Garvey's

Marcus Garvey

Marcus Garvey was called the Black Moses. He wanted to lead black people in the Americas to a new nation of their own in Africa. He was born in Jamaica on August 17, 1887. When his Back to Africa movement failed to catch on there, he moved to the United States in 1916.

Garvey set up his Universal Negro Improvement Association (UNIA) in Harlem, where he lived, and in other northern ghettos. He educated blacks about the accomplishments of black heroes and black culture. He dreamed of a "new Negro" who would be proud of being black.

Garvey's fiery speeches gave voice to the bitterness felt by millions of blacks after the Civil War, which was supposed to have set them free. At his height in 1919 and 1920, he had about two million followers. But he believed so strongly in racial purity that he even approved of white hate groups, such as the Ku Klux Klan, that wanted to keep the races segregated. This angered other black leaders. Garvey's influence died in 1922, when he was convicted of mail fraud linked to a fund-raising campaign and sent to prison.

Garvey was pardoned after two years, but he was forced to leave the country. He never got his movement going again. He was all but forgotten when he died. But his ideas were brought back to life years later by black leaders, including Malcolm X. And Jamaica has proclaimed him a national hero.

Marcus Garvey in ceremonial uniform.

message opened many black people's eyes. After hearing it, they found it hard to be happy scrubbing the floors of white people's homes.

The Reverend Little had been threatened many times for his "uppity" talk, and once angry whites had stormed his house. When Malcolm was still a young child, Earl Little moved his family to Lansing, Michigan. He continued his preaching, and the whites of Lansing didn't like it any better than the whites in Omaha had. Finally, the family's home was burned.

But the violence didn't stop there. One terrible day when Malcolm was 6 years old, his father was found dead. His skull had been crushed and his body cut nearly in half. Local blacks said white men had beaten him and laid him across the streetcar tracks.

The Reverend Little's murder struck Malcolm's mother, Louise, numb with grief. Not only had she lost her husband, but now she had to provide for Malcolm and his sister and brothers all by herself.

Louise got jobs doing housework and sewing for white people. But she never kept a job long. When her bosses found out who her husband had been, they let her go every time. The family sank into poverty. Sometimes the children got dizzy from hunger. Louise fed them boiled dandelion greens, so they wouldn't starve. Neighbors teased the Littles for eating "fried grass."

After a few years, Louise broke down completely. She would sit and stare at nothing for hours. She talked to herself. The house became messy. The children weren't looked after. They sensed something bad was coming.

When Malcolm was 12, state social workers took him away to live with another family. He had been stealing from stores. They said he needed better care. Soon the other children were taken too, and Louise was put in a mental hospital.

Malcolm liked his new family, but he missed his mother. He slid into bad habits and got into trouble at school. The day he put a tack on his teacher's chair, it was the last straw. He was expelled from school and sent to a detention home.

As it turned out, a very nice white couple, the Swerlins, ran the home. Malcolm had his own room for the first time, and he was allowed to enroll in the local junior high school. There were only a few other black students in the school, but the white students were very friendly.

Malcolm hardly noticed it at the time, but later he realized something about the Swerlins and his new school. Everyone liked him, but they treated him more like a pet than like another human being. They didn't think twice about using the word "nigger" in front of him—as if he weren't there. One of Malcolm's teachers even made "nigger" jokes in class.

During World War II, blacks protested segregation in the military.

Malcolm was a bright child and did very well in school. He also played on the basketball team, and later he was even elected class president. He didn't let the racial insults bother him.

When he grew up, he understood why. "I didn't really have much feeling about being a negro," he said, "because I was trying so hard, in every way I could, to be white."

Restless

Malcolm's life changed when his half-sister, Ella, came to visit. She was his father's grown daughter from a previous marriage. When Ella invited the 15-year-old Malcolm to spend the summer at her home in Boston, he jumped at the chance.

Malcolm and his sister, Ella.

Ella lived in Sugar Hill, a middle-class neighborhood in Roxbury, a black section of Boston. Malcolm was amazed at how many black people crowded the streets at night. Everything about the place thrilled him: the neon lights, the bars and pool halls, the rich smells of "down home" black cooking.

When Malcolm got back to Michigan, he felt restless around the white people he had accepted before. Everyone noticed a change in him. The difference was pride: For the first time, Malcolm felt proud to be black.

Around this time, something happened that Malcolm would never forget. Mr. Ostrowski, his favorite teacher, asked him what he planned to do with his life. Malcolm hadn't really thought about it. But he suddenly found himself saying, "I've been thinking I'd like to be a lawyer."

Mr. Ostrowski sat back and smiled. "Malcolm," he said, "…we all here like you.… But you've got to be realistic about being a nigger. A lawyer—that's no realistic goal for a nigger."

The things Mr. Ostrowski said made Malcolm feel worse than ever. He became sullen, and the Swerlins eventually decided that he didn't like living with them at the detention home anymore. They found a family for him. Malcolm stayed with the new family until he finished eighth grade. Then he moved to Boston to live with Ella. But he never told anyone what was wrong.

Hipster

Malcolm learned quickly that he didn't much like the "Hill Negroes" in Ella's neighborhood. They put on airs, pretending to be better than the ghetto blacks down the road. Malcolm was lured to the streets of the ghetto, with their storefront churches, bars, and pawnshops. He admired the sharply dressed "cats" he found there. He learned their "hip" slang. A friend helped him find a "slave"—a job—shining shoes

*Malcolm in
his zoot suit.*

at the Roseland Ballroom, where all the big bands played. When Malcolm first saw the wide wooden dance floor and felt the throbbing music and the rumble of the stomping feet, he thought he was in heaven.

Soon Malcolm bought his first "zoot suit"—the big, baggy, wild-colored outfits that were in style at the time. His was purple. Then he got his first "conk." This was a hairdo that involved rubbing a mixture of lye into his scalp—which stung like mad! His once kinky hair flopped on his forehead, all ropy and straight. He oiled it and slicked it back high, just like the other black "cats" who wanted to look white.

By the time Malcolm was 16, he was over six feet tall and could pass for a "hipster" of 21. He began drinking and taking drugs. Ella didn't like the way Malcolm was changing. She was glad when he got a job on the railroad. She hoped it would get him out of town, away from the crowd he was running with. But Malcolm was looking for new crowds. He found them in Harlem, the black section of New York City. Harlem was so big and exciting that it made Roxbury seem like a sandbox.

Malcolm was fired from his job on the railroad for smart-mouthing customers. He moved to Harlem and went to work as a waiter in a Harlem night club. For a while, he was happy just soaking up the atmosphere. But then he lost his job at the club, and instead of getting another job he decided to "hustle."

Of all the people Malcolm met in Harlem, the hustlers fascinated him most: the con men, bookies, gamblers, and pickpockets. He admired how they lived by their wits. He decided *his* hustle would be selling "reefers," or marijuana.

Malcolm made money selling drugs and spent it on gambling and high living. But he had become, as he later saw, "an animal," living by the laws of the jungle. He began to fear people were after him—the police, other hustlers. He started to carry a gun. Worse, he knew that if he was cornered, he would kill.

Malcolm moved from one hustle to another, but his fast life was catching up to him. Another hustler was said to be gunning for him. He fled to Boston and his old friends, and he taught them some new tricks. Before long, he and his friends were arrested for a string of burglaries.

At the age of 21, when some men graduate from college, Malcolm Little went to Charlestown State Prison. He had been given a ten-year sentence.

Malcolm X

Malcolm's first weeks in prison were awful. Without drugs to feed his habit, his mood was foul. He broke prison rules and was punished by being put in "solitary"—a cell even tinier and filthier than his regular one. Then Malcolm would shout curses at the world and at God. Guards started calling him Satan.

After a while, Malcolm calmed down. His luck changed. He met an inmate who got him interested in books. Malcolm had been an excellent student once. He decided to try again and signed up for classes at the prison. He checked out all kinds of books from the prison library.

As Malcolm read and learned, rays of light pierced the fog in his mind. Then one day, his younger brother, Reginald, came to visit. Reginald told Malcolm about a religion he had joined. He called it Islam. But it wasn't really. Islam is a religion practiced by Muslims the world over. Reginald was talking about a religion called the Nation of Islam, which was started by blacks in America and which was modeled on Islam.

The leader of the Nation of Islam was a frail, quiet black man who called himself Elijah Muhammad after the Islamic prophet Muhammad. Elijah Muhammad taught blacks that "the white man" was "the Devil." For centuries, he said, the white devil had oppressed blacks with violence and deception. And he had been so successful that the black man had forgotten who he really was.

This photo was taken before Malcolm went to prison.

Islam

Islam is the major religion in much of Asia, Africa, the Middle East, Pakistan, Malaysia, and Indonesia. The word "islam" is Arabic. It means "surrender." The basic belief of the Islamic faith is that followers, called Muslims, must surrender to the will of God, which can be learned by reading the Koran.

The Koran is the book of holy scriptures revealed by God to the prophet Muhammad, who lived in the seventh century A.D. It is written in Arabic, the language used in Islam the world over. That is why Muslims refer to God as Allah, his Arabic name. They believe Muhammad was the last and greatest of God's prophets. Other prophets include Adam, Noah, Abraham, Moses, and Jesus. Muslims also accept the holy books of other religions, including Christianity and Judaism, as the words of God. But the Koran is God's final word.

Muslims have five basic duties, called the Five Pillars of Islam.

1. At least once in their lives they must say, "There is no god but God, and Muhammad is His prophet."
2. They must pray facing the holy city of Mecca, in Saudi Arabia, five times daily.
3. They must generously give "alms"—money for the poor.
4. They must fast and pray during Ramadan, the ninth month of the Muslim calendar.
5. And if possible, once in their lives, they must make a pilgrimage to Mecca.

The so-called Black Muslims of the Nation of Islam observed some Islamic rites. But many of their doctrines, such as the belief in the "white devil," were based on race and are not part of Islam.

This is a page of the Koran, the Islamic holy book, written in Arabic.

Africans were captured by Europeans and sold into slavery.

Elijah Muhammad taught that blacks were members of the "original" race, that blacks had built great civilizations and empires in Africa and Asia while whites were still living in caves. Then whites had grown powerful by enslaving the dark races of the world.

According to Elijah Muhammad, the white slave master took everything away from the black man: his freedom, his knowledge of his own glorious past, even his name. The slave master stamped his own name on his slave, as if the slave were a piece of property.

Reginald told Malcolm of Elijah Muhammad's teachings. Malcolm later said they hit him "like a blinding light." Malcolm read even more than before, and now he read with a purpose. He wanted to see if the things Reginald said were true.

Elijah Muhammad

Malcolm read that white Europeans began the slave trade, kidnapping and slaughtering millions of innocent black Africans. He read that whites colonized Africa, Asia, and South America, exploiting the native, dark-skinned peoples to enrich themselves. He found enough evidence to convince himself that everything Reginald had told him was true: The white man *was* the devil.

Malcolm thought about how, in his own life, the white man had been devilish. He recalled how his home had been burned and his father murdered by white men, how his classmates had called him "nigger," how his teacher had told him to forget about becoming a lawyer. He decided that he and other blacks turned to crime because society gave them no chance to better themselves.

When Malcolm was 27, he was released from prison on parole. He moved to Detroit and joined the Nation of Islam. Following the practices of the Nation, he gave up his "slave" name and was given an X in its place. From then on he would be called Malcolm X.

"Hate-Teachers"

Malcolm was not prepared for the wave of emotions he felt when he finally met Elijah Muhammad and heard him speak. "I worshiped him," he later said.

Elijah Muhammad's followers in the Nation of Islam also impressed Malcolm. They observed a strict moral code. Smoking and drinking weren't allowed. Nation members treated one another with affection

Black Muslims protest the arrest of two of their members.

and respect. They took pride in their black heritage. They also encouraged blacks to buy from businesses run by other blacks, so their money would not be drained from the ghetto to enrich the white man. The Nation even set up its own restaurants and markets as examples of well-run black enterprises. Eventually, they wanted blacks to have their own country, either in Africa or somewhere within the United States.

Malcolm now saw the black people on ghetto streets with new eyes. He felt that they had been "brainwashed" by the white man, as he had been, to hate their true selves. He now understood that he had conked his hair because he hated his blackness, and that he drank and took drugs to escape from himself.

Malcolm soon began visiting the ghettos to recruit new members to the Detroit temple. His experiences as a hustler helped. "I knew the thinking and the language of the ghetto streets," he said.

Malcolm was invited to speak to an assembly of Nation members. When he talked about what Elijah Muhammad's teachings had done for him, the power of truth was in his words. "If I told you the life I have lived, you would find it hard to believe me," he said. And, indeed, he had become a new man.

Malcolm's talent as a speaker and the knowledge he had gained in prison impressed those who heard him speak. He was soon named a minister of the Nation of Islam. In time, he became Elijah Muhammad's main spokesman.

Malcolm's fiery speeches held audiences rapt. "The white man wants black men to stay immoral, unclean and ignorant," he said, in that cocksure, wised-up way of his that made black people happy and angry at the same time. "As long as we stay in these conditions, we will keep on begging him and he will control us."

Malcolm helped recruit members to new temples in Boston and Philadelphia. He did such a good job that he was named minister of the temple in Harlem, where he faced the challenge of bringing the Nation's message to the more than one million blacks in New York City.

Malcolm's preaching struck a chord in Harlem's blacks. He quickly became a force in the community. Just how strong a force became clear one night when a black man was beaten by a white policeman and thrown in jail. Malcolm learned that the man was seriously injured and needed medical care. Malcolm contacted his people and asked them to meet him at the police station. Soon, more than two thousand of his followers had gathered. They kept a silent vigil outside the station, demanding only that the man be seen by doctors. Fearing a riot, the police gave in. Then, Mal-

*Malcolm X at home with
his wife and daughters.*

colm simply waved his hand, and the crowd vanished. The police were stunned.

So was Harlem. Word spread quickly about how Malcolm X had made the police do what he wanted. The nerve of it! People in Harlem admired his leadership. Malcolm's stature grew rapidly, and so did membership in his temple.

In 1958, Malcolm married a woman who belonged to the Harlem temple, Sister Betty, a nurse who taught hygiene to Nation members. They eventually had four daughters. Malcolm loved his family, but his work always dominated his life. He put in long hours, preaching and teaching. He even started a newspaper, *Muhammad Speaks*, to help spread the word.

Though the Nation was growing, very few whites had heard of it. That changed in late 1959. A TV network did a show about the Nation, called "The Hate that Hate Produced." Millions of people, black and white, saw and heard the fiery young minister, Malcolm X, condemn the "white devil."

Malcolm X's speeches drew large and enthusiastic crowds.

Malcolm X and Martin Luther King, Jr.

The reaction was swift. Newspapers and magazines across the country wrote angry stories about the Black Muslims, as Nation members were called. They were labeled "hate-teachers" and "black racists." Malcolm was surrounded by reporters who asked him to explain his teachings. He enjoyed sparring with them. "The white man is in no moral position to accuse anyone else of hate," he told them.

Reporters pointed to the struggles of the civil rights movement led by Dr. Martin Luther King, Jr. The movement had broken down legal barriers that kept blacks from riding buses alongside whites and going to the same schools that whites attended. King used peaceful sit-ins and marches to win his victories. Wasn't that more useful, they asked Malcolm, than teaching hate?

Malcolm scoffed. He said the reason white people liked King was that he "controlled" blacks and kept them "on the plantation."

Malcolm criticized King's nonviolent methods. He said that black people who were attacked by whites should not "turn the other cheek" but should defend themselves. He even said blacks should buy guns. When such statements made whites nervous, Malcolm became angry. They would never panic, he said, if he called for *white* people to buy guns to defend themselves.

Oddly, the more Malcolm was feared, the more TV and radio stations wanted him on their shows. The young minister became much better known than the quiet Elijah Muhammad. This soon caused problems.

Some in the Nation of Islam said Malcolm was trying to upstage their leader. At first, Elijah Muhammad ignored such suggestions. But then, after he had ordered all his ministers not to make any statements about the assassination of President John Kennedy in November 1963, Malcolm spoke out anyway. Elijah Muhammad suspended Malcolm from the ministry.

After this, troubles between Malcolm and the Nation grew more intense. In time, Malcolm began to hear rumors that he didn't want to believe—that Elijah Muhammad wanted him killed. The idea that his beloved leader hated him so much pained Malcolm deeply.

Malcolm X and the Nation of Islam could not mend their differences. Though Malcolm was still devoted to Elijah Muhammad, he resigned from the Nation in March 1964. He was on his own.

Mecca

Malcolm kept on preaching and teaching. But his message changed in April 1964, after he took a trip to the holy city of Mecca in Saudi Arabia, the center of the Islamic faith.

In Mecca, Malcolm learned Islamic ideas of brotherhood and love. His teacher, a devout Muslim, was also a white man. Malcolm learned how Elijah Muhammad had changed Islamic teachings to suit himself.

Pilgrims seated at the Ka'aba *(sacred shrine) in Mecca.*

He saw that the holy city was filled with faithful Muslims, both black and white, who treated one another with grace and affection. He realized that white people weren't all devils, and that peace and understanding among all peoples was the highest goal. Malcolm joined the traditional Muslims. They gave him a new name, El Hajj Malik El-Shabazz.

When he returned home, Malcolm spoke about how he had changed. Many people didn't believe him. He still rejected integration—having blacks and whites live and work together—as a way to help blacks get ahead. But he no longer thought that blacks should go back to Africa. He wanted them to take pride in their race, to respect and help themselves. He urged them not to "beg" for civil rights, but to demand "human rights."

Malcolm traveled to Africa and met with the heads of many nations. They treated him as if he were a visiting prince. He asked for their help to force the United Nations to take action against the United States for violating the human rights of black Americans.

When he arrived back home, Malcolm had fresh ideas and new hopes. He wanted to find a way to work with the leaders of the civil rights movement. But he never got the chance.

On February 21, 1965, Malcolm went to the Audubon Ballroom in Harlem to speak to his followers. He looked tired and worried. Ever since he had left the Nation, there had been threats against his life. He assumed the threats were from followers of Elijah Muhammad. Malcolm felt sure that he would soon die by violence.

When Malcolm walked into the ballroom and greeted the audience, four armed men stood up, raised guns, and fired at him. Malcolm fell back on the stage. As he lay there, wounded and bleeding, the men kept firing bullets into his body.

Malcolm was dead before he could be taken to the hospital. The police arrested three members of the Nation of Islam, who were sent to prison for his murder. The fourth gunman was never found.

When Malcolm X was alive, many said he accomplished little compared to the patient protesters of the civil rights movement. But after his death, a book called *The Autobiography of Malcolm X* was

published. The writer Alex Haley had worked with Malcolm to tell the story of his life. After Malcolm's death, the book spelled out for millions what

The Audubon Ballroom today.

was clear to those who had known Malcolm X: His life's greatest achievement was how he lived it.

The civil rights movement sought to change unjust laws and win legal rights for blacks. But Malcolm X wanted to change the unjust laws written on black people's souls. He believed the greatest crime com-

Malcolm X's grave in Hartsdale, New York.

mitted against blacks was that they were taught to hate themselves. Malcolm X wanted to free the souls of blacks from self-hatred—to make them proud. But first he had to free himself from the self-hatred of drug abuse, crime, and bad living, and learn to discipline his body and mind.

Belief in Malcolm X's messages of black pride and self-help is more widespread today than when he was alive. At his funeral, Ossie Davis, the actor, expressed why people would treasure his memory for years to come:

"Malcolm was our manhood, our living black manhood.... In honoring him, we honor the best in ourselves."

Important Events in the Life of Malcolm X

1925	Malcolm Little is born on May 19 in Omaha, Nebraska.
1940	Malcolm goes to live with his half-sister, Ella, in Boston.
1942	Malcolm moves to Harlem, New York.
1946	Malcolm is imprisoned for robbery.
1952	Following his release from prison, Malcolm joins the Nation of Islam and changes his name to Malcolm X.
1954	Malcolm becomes minister of a Muslim temple in Harlem.
1958	Malcolm marries Sister Betty.
1963	Malcolm is suspended from his ministry by Elijah Muhammad.
1964	Malcolm breaks with the Nation of Islam and forms his own Muslim organization, Muslim Mosque, Inc.
	Malcolm makes a pilgrimage to Mecca.
1965	Malcolm X is shot to death on February 21 at the Audubon Ballroom in Harlem, New York.

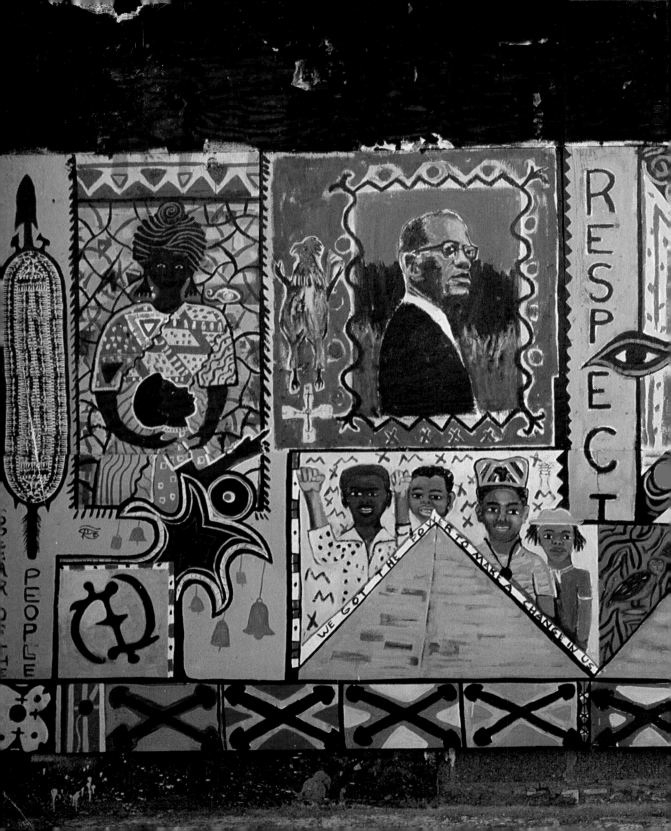

RESPECT

PEOPLE

WE GOT THE POWER TO MAKE A CHANGE IN US

Find Out More About Malcolm X

Books: *Islam* by Abdul Latif Al Hood (New York: Bookwright Press, 1987).

Malcolm X by Arnold Adoff (New York: Harper Junior, 1988).

Malcolm X: Black & Proud by Florence M. White (Champaign, Ill.: Garrard, 1975).

The Picture Life of Malcolm X by James Haskins (New York: Franklin Watts, 1975).

Places: The Audubon Ballroom is in New York City, at 165th Street and Broadway.

Images of black pride are painted on the walls of the Audubon Ballroom, where Malcolm X was killed.

Index